Nature Explorers

Forests
and Woods

Nick Baker

Collins
An Imprint of HarperCollinsPublishers

For my wild friend Ceri, a small token of my appreciation of you. You saved me!

ISBN: 978-0-00-720765-7
ISBN-10: 0-00-720765-4

www.harpercollins.com

ISBN: 978-0-06-089078-0 (in the United States)
ISBN-10: 0-06-089078-9

FIRST U.S. EDITION Published in 2007.
HarperCollins books may be purchased
for educational, business, or sales promotional use. For
information in the United States, please write to:
Special Markets Department, HarperCollins Publishers,
10 East 53rd Street, New York, NY 10022.

The name of the "Smithsonian," "Smithsonian
Institution," and the sunburst logo are registered
trademarks of the Smithsonian Institution.

Text © Nick Baker 2007
Photographer: Nikki English, except for those pictures credited on page 71
Flick book illustrations: Lizzie Harper
Colour reproduction by Dot Gradations Ltd, UK
Printed and bound by Printing Express, Hong Kong

10 09 08 07
7 6 5 4 3 2 1

Disclaimer: Many of the projects in this book involve tools, knives, fire, or cooking. All of these can be dangerous and require a good deal of training and practice before they are safely used. Parents should supervise these activities and monitor the correct use of tools until children can be considered competent to use them themselves. In addition, common sense and basic precautions—knowing exactly where your children are and what they are doing at all times, making sure they wear sunscreen and appropriate, protective clothing, and teaching them how to respect nature and safely explore their surroundings—are the key to your children learning the joys of the great outdoors.

Contents

Flick the pages to see the leaf move!

The wildlife in the woods

Looking up through the bright green, newly unfurled leaves of beech woods, you may feel as though you are in a huge cathedral gazing up through the stained glass windows—ones that are made up of many shades of green. But we chop these trees down, use them as crops, or as things to climb. Woods are places to walk the dog, they form barriers and boundaries, but they are the lungs of the planet.

Trees are amazing light machines. Just like other plants, they trap the Sun's energy by using it to combine water and carbon dioxide gas in the air to form sugars. But trees do it on a much bigger scale. Each one is a light factory, with tiny microscopic work stations inside each leaf. While looking up through the canopy, hold a leaf in your hand and imagine the scale of production. Think of the millions of little cells in the leaf and then multiply by the number of leaves you can see all around you. An acre of woods is such an effective factory that it produces over 5,000 tons of roots, wood, and leaves every year!

To smaller beasts, a field of grass is like a forest, but a forest, woods, or copse is a unique experience for human-sized creatures. This is exactly what this book is about: exploring our woods, forests, hedgerows, and some of the habitats that are associated with them.

The book is divided into chapters that roughly reflect the different levels of woods. Imagine the woods as if they were a layer cake. If you were able to take a slice through them, you would see a pattern to the apparent tangled mass of life.

The tree canopy. This is the icing on the cake. In mature woods this can be quite dense and it affects the sorts of animals and plants that live below. Because getting a feel for canopies is quite hard, we explore the older trees and see what we can learn from them.

The understory. This is the next layer down and is made up of younger trees or shrubs and can be thicker on the edges of woods and forests. In woods that have recently been cleared, this may be the only vegetation you've got.

The herb layer. Made up of plants that are not woody, such as ferns, grasses and wildflowers, you are now nearing the bottom of the woods.

The litter layer. This is the lowest of the layers, right at the bottom, and it is where most living things in the woods or hedge end up.

Handy stuff for exploring

As a youthful naturalist with, I assume, little pocket money, you will be relieved to know that when it comes to specialist equipment, there really isn't much needed! Most can be put together and constructed or improvized from items found under the sink, in the shed, or under the stairs. In fact, the most important tools you need to learn to use are your own senses; but more about that later. For now, though, here is a short list of things that I find useful in an everyday kind of way when exploring the woods.

Bamboo garden canes These are handy things for many of the activities in this book and they are useful for creating an extension to your arms! You can tape a wire hook to the end and use it to bend down branches that were otherwise out of your reach or use it to beat branches that are in your way.

Binoculars and magnifying lens Anything with a lens in it to magnify little things or bring distant subjects closer is going to be a relatively expensive bit of kit compared with the rest of the equipment you might have with you. But if you can possibly afford it, they are really worth investing in and there are many different kinds at prices to suit all budgets.

Clear plastic containers These can be anything from specially-made specimen vials to old 35mm film canisters and empty jam jars. They are handy for collecting and observing specimens. Plastic bags are also very useful and have the added advantage of being lightweight and folding flat in your pocket.

Duct tape Many of the things you build or construct in this book use this wonderful stuff. It is also excellent for making repairs and quick fixes.

Large
strainer

Pens and
pencils

Duct tape

Bamboo
canes

Field
guides

Binoculars

Clear plastic
containers

Plastic bags

Backpack

Field guides Always handy, but if you take good notes, they can be consulted once you get home and so save you space in your pockets or your day pack.

First aid kit Keep a fully equipped kit close by at all times, including insect repellent, sunscreen, antiseptic spray, and band aids.

Pen and notebook It is essential to record your observations, never mind how seemingly insignificant they may be. All the best naturalists do it.

Strainer Useful for panning through leaf litter and soil. This is one of the best ways to find the over-wintering pupae of many moth species.

Backpack Finally, you need something to put all this stuff in! Make sure it's large enough to carry everything, but that it's not so heavy it spoils a day out in the woods.

The tree canopy

A tree on its own is never a tree on its own. Trees act like a life magnet. You can have a plain bare patch of grass with nothing much in the way of wildlife hanging around. But stick a tree in the middle of it and it's a whole different story. Birds will perch in it and may nest there, insects will find it attractive and nibble, or even breed, in it. As the tree gets bigger, it creates more living space for even more life.

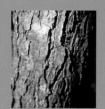

Making an inventory of a tree near you is always a fun thing to do, and would be a great idea for a personal project or something you can do at school. Try to count as many living things as you can, from the microscopic algae that give the cracks in the bark a greenish tinge, to the birds and mammals that visit. You will be very surprised at what you find.

But just imagine what happens when you stick a collection of these incredible trees together! The effect is magnified, which is why woodlands are such amazing places to explore and why some people make such a fuss when they get removed.

This chapter is about the trees themselves—what they are, how they live and grow. Get to know the trees and you will begin to understand and love the heart of the wood itself.

Fab facts

Here are some BIG numbers for some oak woodlands:
* 100 acres of woodland can support 300-400 birds.
* 30 different types of lichen are found on the bark of some trees.
* 200 species of moth caterpillars feed on the leaves.
* 45 true bugs suck its juices and stalk other prey among its branches.
* 65 mosses and liverworts can be found on the bark.
* 40 species of galls have been found on oak trees.

A chewed acorn may end up on the woodland floor, but while it's alive, it grows much further up a tree, near the tree canopy.

A gray squirrel's drey, neatly perched high in the canopy.

The dappled sunshine emerging through the tree canopy is always a cheering sight.

Are your woods old?

Many woodlands and forests have been a feature of our landscape for a long time while others have been cleared and have either been re-colonized or re-planted. While all woodlands offer shelter and food for certain creatures, those that have been around for longer tend to have a greater number of species. This variety of species is called biodiversity.

In the spring, investigate your local woodland. Is it ablaze with color before the leaves come out, as a carpet of plants explode into flower and leaf on the forest floor? There is only a brief window of warmth and light in a wood before the leafy canopy closes over and returns most of the wood floor into the dappled half light. This is why so many plants in the understory have broad leaves (see also opposite).

We humans have real trouble thinking outside of our own life expectancy. We tend to think that we are doing well if we get to 80 years old, but many trees at 80 are still young. Living at a slower speed than us is part of their fascination. As long-lived plants, they have their own stories to tell. They are like living history lessons, telling us about their own lives and the conditions to which they were exposed as they grew.

Get to know some of the truly old trees in your area. Work out their age (see pages 18–19 and the Take it further box, opposite) and learn about their history; perhaps relate it to famous historical events in human history, such as wars and invasions. You will soon get a sense of what events these trees may have stood through. This is the first step to tree appreciation and helps you to enjoy them fully. You might also help a little by planting a few of your own (see pages 24–5).

Look closely at many spring-flowering plants. They often have large, broad leaves designed to absorb as much of the sparse light that falls on them as possible. Many also grow in large and dense mats, a sign that they reproduce and spread mainly by bulb splitting and underground runners, rather than by seeding. The fact that they spread like this means they tend to be specialized at surviving in woodlands but are next to useless at spreading to new locations. As a result, they take many years to colonize a woodland.

Woods were once used as a crop and their products were used in day-to-day life. Look for multi-trunked trees that seem to grow from a thick and gnarly old base. These may well have been cut at some time. In historical times cut poles from young trees were used for building poles or for making fences, while others would be burnt to produce charcoal for blacksmiths and home fires. Today, coppicing still goes on in some woods.

Take it further

* Other clues to the age and use of a woodland can be found by looking for tell-tale traces of how man has managed them.

* Old woods tend to have uneven and curved boundaries while new ones are usually straighter.

* Plants are another great way to tell if a woodland is old or undisturbed. Look for:

trilliums and other members of the lily family, violets, hepaticas, blood root orchids, and woodland asters.

Keep a tree log

Starting to identify trees can be a little daunting. Some are easier to tell apart than others. For example, pine and spruce trees have cones and needles and they keep their leaves all year round. Deciduous trees like oaks and maples have big flat leaves that turn brown, yellow, and red and fall off in the winter. But learning about trees in more depth can be complicated. To help, make your own tree log. This is an excellent way to collect as much information as possible about the trees in your area, and you can start at any time of the year.

The first characteristic to look for in your tree is the shape of the leaves. Each species has its own distinctive leaf pattern. Most can be identified from this quality alone, although there are a few that you may find a little tricky, such as ashes and elms, and the exotic species introduced from other countries, but you will soon get the hang of the main native species.

Start by collecting a selection of leaves, either from the ground or directly from the tree itself. Once you have these leaves back at home there are several ways you can incorporate them into your log—start with the ideas opposite and more are given on the following pages. You can then move onto exploring the bark (see pages 16–17), seeing how old it is (pages 18–19), and drawing its profile (pages 20–21).

To make your tree log, use a scrap book or collect some loose pages or some clear plastic pockets. You can keep adding to your file as you find more information and evidence.

2 Carefully paint over the leaf, just going over its edges. Let it dry.

3 Slowly lift the leaf and, hey presto!, you are left with a perfect outline of your leaf.

1 Use your leaf like a stencil. Place it on paper and fix the stem with tape.

4 You can also use a stiff brush to apply some dark shoe polish to one side of your leaf. Dead leaves that have fallen from a tree work best for this approach as they are stronger and more rigid.

5 When it is well covered, turn the leaf over and press it firmly onto a plain sheet of paper to leave an imprint. Press some blotting or kitchen paper over this to soak up any oily residues.

Make leaf lace

If you have been sifting around in the bottom of a pond or ditch, you may occasionally stumble across a stunningly beautiful phenomenon—a leaf that has had all the soft parts nibbled away to leave a net-like web of veins. These veins are all that is left of the leaf's plumbing. The tubes and pipes are what the sap of the plant flows through, carrying essential chemicals around the plant's body.

There is a rather simple and fun way of recreating this effect. Not only are they a beautiful thing to have in your tree log but they can also be mass produced, painted, and used in many creative ways, such as on a collage picture and to decorate cards.

Nick's trick

* Pressing leaves is the same as pressing flowers. You can either use a professional flower press—a stacked sandwich of alternating cardboard and blotting paper between two boards with bolts in each corner—or you can use a heavy book or two to weight down the layers.

* The most important thing is to place your leaf between some absorbent material like blotting paper or paper towel. Sheets of plastic will also stop any plant sap from oozing out and ruining your book cover or pages.

* Change the blotting paper every other day and after a few weeks your leaves will be preserved. I like to store mine in individual plastic envelopes with a label on the outside of each one saying what it is and where the trees were growing.

YOU WILL NEED

> **leaves**
> **baking soda**
> **a pan of water**
> **a soft paint brush**

3 Leave them submerged for a good 30 minutes, making sure all of the leaves are under the surface. Then gently wash the leaves with fresh water by placing the pan under a slowly running cold tap, letting the water flush out the soda mixture and soft debris.

2 Place the pan on a gentle heat until it is simmering, then take the pan away from the heat and place your leaves in the solution.

1 Fill your pan with water and add about 2 tablespoons of baking soda for every 2½ cups of water.

4 You should now be left with beautiful transparent leaves. To remove the soft material surrounding the veins, place the leaves on a saucer and gently brush with an artist's paintbrush. Leave to dry on some paper towel.

The texture of bark

Another distinguishing feature of a tree, and one that remains even in the winter when most leaves have dropped, is the texture of the bark. The quickest and easiest way to record this is to make a rubbing—see Nick's trick, below. The other way of recording your tree requires a little more effort, but it produces a really cool, three-dimensional model of a section of tree trunk—and that is by making a cast of it (see opposite).

Hold the crayon or pastel on its side for the most effective technique. This really helps to bring out the textures underneath.

Nick's trick

* Carefully tape a piece of paper to the trunk of the tree and then color over it with a crayon or pencil (dark looks best on white paper, but white chalk on black paper is pretty effective, also).

* In this way you record all those textures and patterns and soon you will start to recognize a combination of these features and the colors. I have a friend who is a blind naturalist and he can tell most species of tree by these very textures you will be recording with your rubbings.

YOU WILL NEED

> **modeling clay**
> **strong cardboard box**
> **plaster of Paris**
> **water**
> **poster paints**
> **paintbrush**

1 First find the tree you wish to make an impression of. Then knead and pummel your modeling clay so it is soft and free of air bubbles. This makes it much easier to work with and gives you a better impression at the end.

2 Firmly press the clay into the tree's surface. Try to keep the clay more than ⅛ inch thick and aim to keep the edges from tapering. If you are going to make many such casts for a collection, use standard dimensions at this point as it makes the casts easier to store and/or mount.

3 Peel away the clay and you will notice all the bark textures on it. You now have to get this home without damaging the mold, so this is where a stout box to transport the clay comes in handy.

4 Once back home, place the mold with the textured surface uppermost. Then use more modeling clay to make a ridge at least 1 inch higher than the mold. You can choose at this point whether to make a curved cast (see above), like the profile of the tree, or a flat section.

5 Following the packet's instructions, mix some plaster of Paris with water. Pour the plaster into the mold and leave to set for a few hours. Then carefully lift and peel away the modeling clay to leave your bark cast, ready for display.

6 If you like, you can paint your bark impression with poster paints so that it looks even more lifelike.

How old is your tree?

The most accurate way to tell the age of a tree is to look at a slice through its trunk and count the growth rings. The cells under the tree's skin (the bark) produce new wood as the tree grows and each summer, more new cells are made when conditions are best for growth. Growth rings show each year's new growth—one for each year of the tree's life. In years of good growth, the rings will be wider.

Obviously getting to see these growth rings in a healthy tree is impossible without cutting it down and destroying the thing you are studying! But if you come across stumps that have been sawn through and the cut is a smooth one, you should be able to see how old it was when the tree was felled. This will give you an estimated age of any tree of the same species in the same area.

Some trees grow very slowly indeed, but others have many a growth spurt, such as the many pines, various cedars, spruce and fir, poplars, birch, some willows and other non-natives such as eucalyptus. Slower-growing trees include oak, beech, maple, yew, and most smaller-growing trees.

Fab facts

* Trees grow from the outside in! The growth cells are all in the surface of the wood, under the bark. They lay down new wood as the tree trunk expands. The wood in the middle of an old tree is usually dead and when a branch falls off, it is this that sometimes gets hollowed out by fungus and birds.

1 Another way to estimate a tree's age is by measuring the girth of the trunk about 3 feet up. Because large trees tend to grow at a predictable rate, their trunk gets thicker as they grow and on average, trees put on about an inch a year.

2 So measure your tree's girth in inches. You will then have an approximate age for your tree. This is a very rough guess and growth rate does vary from species to species and from place to place.

YOU WILL NEED

> **a tape measure**
> **pencil**
> **paper**
> **calculator**

Take it further

* Try to find a tree stump that shows the tree is at least 100 years old and take a photograph of it.

* Either have the photograph enlarged or enlarge a photocopy. If you have a digital camera, print out the image to whatever size you want. You can then mark important years on the trunk by counting back rings.

* Show the year 2000; the year you were born; the year of the first moon landing, and add anything else that is of interest to you and your family.

Profiling your tree

For any tree, you can create a profile of its shape and height. It is not too hard to figure out the circumference of a tree trunk, you just need to put a tape measure around it, as if you were measuring your own waist (see previous page). But height is a different matter, especially if you are dealing with a large, mature woodland tree. Fear not—it's surprisingly easy (see opposite).

You can also measure and record the shape and size of the tree canopy by drawing the trunk on a piece of graph paper (say, ⅛ inch on the paper equals 3 feet in real life). Pace out to the distances from the trunk to the edge of the canopy as you look up. Repeat all around the tree. Add these distances to your plan on the graph paper.

The size and the shape of the tree can give you a good idea of the way it has grown and the condition it is in. For example, if it is leaning to one side, that might show the most usual wind direction.

Like all living things on Earth, trees need to reproduce, so the last addition to your log will be descriptions of when and how the tree flowers. Look for flowers and seeds and note how they grow. Do they dangle? Are they on short stems or on twigs or old branches? Collect and draw or photograph these for your tree log.

On a paper birch, the seeds hang from the branches on long stems.

Take my advice

Part of your tree profiling could be to get to know the animals and other plants that can be found living in or around your tree.

YOU WILL NEED

> **a friend**
> **pencil**
> **paper**
> **tape measure**

2 Rotate the pencil through 90 degrees, keeping the base of the pencil in line with the base of the tree. Ask your friend to walk away from the tree to the point that corresponds with the tip of your pencil.

3 Ask your friend to mark this spot and then measure the distance between the tree trunk and your friend.

1 Standing some distance away from your chosen tree, hold the pencil up at arm's length. Move backward and forward until the pencil's height is the same as that of the tree.

4 On a piece of paper, note down the distance. It is very important as it equals the height of the tree. Magic!

You will now have a fantastic record of all your tree observations.

Whistling in the woods

Here's a project that will give you a real buzz. Just by whittling a piece of maple, it's possible to make something that whistles in a really cool way. But first you have to identify a maple. These trees are very common in deciduous woods and have large flat leaves with several points on them. Think Canadian flag and that is a maple leaf (see left and page 29). Other easy-to-identify features are the seeds or keys, which are the famous paired winged seeds that work a little like a helicopter (see page 52).

1 Get an adult to help you cut a 6 inch length of maple branch that is about the same diameter as your finger. It is easier to make if you let the twig dry out a little for a couple of days.

3 About half an inch down the twig cut a small slot in the bark, making sure you have cut right through the smooth bark and scored the wood below.

4 Now for the tricky bit— tap and loosen the bark at the top of the whistle and slip the bark off in one piece.

2 About an inch down the twig, use your knife to score right around the middle.

5 Where you scored through to the wood below, cut out a thin section of wood. Don't make it too deep.

6 Slide the bark back over the twig, lining up the hole in the bark with the hole in the wood. Now blow!

Grow your own giant

Growing your own tree is a great way to learn all about seeds, trees, and the different ways they grow, and at the end of it you will have a small woodland developing right before your eyes (see opposite)! You can then either plant the seedlings or give them away as presents to friends and relatives. First, though, you will need to collect your seeds. Different trees have different kinds of seeds, but the easiest are those that simply drop off the tree as they do not need any special conditions. Examples are oaks and their acorns, hickory, and maples and ashes, which have winged seeds called "keys."

Most trees produce their seeds in the fall of the year, so set out on an autumn day and try to beat the squirrels, especially to acorns, which they collect off the tree as they start to go brown.

Seeds that are inside a berry have to be treated differently because they are designed to be attractive to birds who swallow the berry, seeds and all. They then pass through the bird's gut and land in the bird's droppings later. This helps the seeds spread away from the parent plant and also gives the seed its own little dollop of fertilizer to get it off to a good start. Species such as holly and cherry are good examples of trees that use this technique. To get these to grow you need to put the seeds through some rough treatment to replicate the guts of a bird—see Step 5.

Fab facts

* A mature oak tree produces around 90,000 acorns a year, but on average only one of these will make it to being a full-grown tree!

* Keep an eye open for blue jays, as they are great fans of the acorn. These birds even bury acorns for future use—sometimes weeks or even months later.

* A little acorn that is developing during the summer is known as a nubbin—what a great word!

> **small flower pots**
> **small stones**
> **peat-free potting soil**
> **seeds**
> **labels**

1 Place some stones or broken bits of tile in the bottom of each pot to help it drain, then fill the rest with potting soil.

2 Make a hole in the center of the soil, about half a finger's depth.

3 Place a seed or nut into the hole and cover with compost. Label each pot so that you don't forget which tree is in which container. Water the pots thoroughly.

4 Store the pots somewhere like a potting shed or garage over the winter, where they will stay cool. This will stimulate them to germinate in the spring. Be aware that mice will not only visit their own stores for the winter but will happily eat any other seeds they stumble upon with their keen sense of smell. So make sure your seeds do not get swiped by the seed stealers! Keep your soil damp, but not too wet.

5 If you collect some holly berries, or cherries, remove the fruit, then wash off the seeds and let them dry out. Put the seeds in a pot with a mixture of sand and peat-free soil and leave out for the winter. Come the spring, plant the seeds in a seed tray. They will start to shoot and you can watch a 'woodland' spring up before your very eyes. Some trees, like oak, are quite slow growing, others are much faster. Re-pot them as they grow.

The understory

Underneath the tree canopy comes the understory, which provides cover for larger animals, such as deer and foxes, as well as smaller creatures, such as woodland birds and, of course, small mammals. The understory is formed by smaller woody plants and it varies in density and abundance, depending on just how much light gets down from above.

If your woodland is a light and breezy place, then more of the woody plants, such as witch hazel, mountain laurel and viburnum, will thrive. But if your woodland is a super dark and dense conifer forest, you may be able to move freely without getting your clothes snagged on brambles or tangly thickets.

The advantage of the understory to the naturalist is that because of the relatively short height of the understory vegetation, the life that lives in it isn't so far away. So being able to see what goes on is much easier than developing neck ache looking into the very tops of the canopy.

In the spring, it is the understory that provides a home for some of the best singers in the dawn chorus. Here birds can claim territories and not have to worry too much about being seen by predators. If they do sing from a perch, it is only a short hop down into thick cover. This, of course, makes seeing anything that lives here a little frustrating, but with lots of patience and by moving around quietly, the understory will eventually yield its secrets.

A good place to look for a nest is in the fork of a tree.

The wood thrush is a bird that spends almost all of its life skulking around in the dense scrub. Hence it is more often heard than seen.

The white-footed mouse is an active nocturnal denizen of the understory as well as the forest floor and has a broad diet that includes nuts, berries, and caterpillars.

Here you can see clearly the understory. But be aware that it isn't always quite as obvious as in this picture.

Brilliant budding

If you are a little impatient for spring and the winter has felt like a long one, this is how you can speed up spring and watch an amazing transformation at the same time.

Toward the end of winter take a short walk along a hedgerow and collect a few of the tips of living branches of some of the species of tree and shrub you find. Species with obvious buds, such as sycamore, ash, and horse chestnut, are the best and most spectacular. When you get home place your finds in a jam jar of water and put them on a bright, warm window sill.

Here you can see a mountain ash, ash, and paper birch. When looking at your buds, ask yourself are they tiny and round or long and sharp? Is the twig narrow and slender or quite thick? Are there clusters of buds at the shoot tip or do they come out at the sides? What color are they? Are they sticky or hairy?

Fab facts

* Trees in the understory burst into leaf earlier than those in the canopy as the sap doesn't have as far to travel. Logical really.

* Look closely at a twig and you will notice small details. Little bumps on the surface are pores known as lenticels. These let gasses in and out of the growing tissues.

* You may also notice small scars where last year's leaves fell off. Look closer still and you may see lots of tiny holes in the surface of these. These are the disconnected ends of the departed leaves' plumbing.

You do not have to wait until spring to see the magic of bright, brand new leaves. Just follow the tips in the box below.

Take it further

* Keep a close eye on your buds. Each one contains one of the best wrapped surprises in nature. Inside is a miniature crumpled collection of leaves and even a stem; some will also contain flowers.

* Just take the buds of horse chestnut or buck-eye. They are covered in a sticky, leathery, protective coating designed to deter those creatures that may want to open these parcels before their time.

* But as your buds swell, you will be able to watch them split and the scales separate. Eventually, the bud is levered out of the way and drops off, leaving a bud scar. This upheaval is caused by the pressure of the swelling, soft green new growth within.

* The leaves then continue to unfurl. Starting off like a crumpled green umbrella they soon expand to their final size. As they do so, the light yellowy green color matures and darkens as a substance called chlorophyll inside the leaves kicks into action and the process known as photosynthesis gets under way.

* With some species, especially those of the willow family, your twigs may end up sprouting roots. Why not keep these? Use them or plant them to grow bonsai.

Mapping territories

What birds say to one another when they sing is along the lines of "Stay off my patch," "I'm the boss here," and "Come over here and breed with me!" Mostly what we think of as cheery, happy music, to birds is really a war of the whistles. They are competing with each other and claiming their little slice of the world.

In the spring, when the breeding season gets under way, these territorial songs are particularly loud and obvious. This is especially the case first thing in the morning, when their singing is called the "dawn chorus."

People often ask me how they can get to know the calls of all these different kinds of birds. My answer is to get out there and start looking and listening. Sure, various identification CDs will help, but there is no better way to get birds and their songs committed to memory than to actually see them singing. Once you have got familiar with the basic songs, test yourself. If you hear a bird singing, make a bold decision and then go looking to see if you were right.

Another way to get to know your local birds and also to get a better understanding of their lives, is to make a bird journal and map—see opposite.

The American robin is a star singer in the dawn chorus.

Take my advice

* The difficulty of learning bird song is sometimes down to the fact that many different species will insist on all singing at the same time! Is that a house wren over there? Could that be a cardinal? And then a mocking bird starts up at the same time as a robin and really confuses and distracts your mind and your ears!

* The best bet is to start early in the year, because in that way you get familiar with the resident birds, the ones that have spent all winter with you. Then by the time all those exotic little colorful birds—the warblers—start to return from warmer climes, you will be ready for them. You will notice the new songs and because you have already got the others sorted out, you can concentrate on the newcomers.

* Do not worry, even the most experienced bird watcher has to relearn some of the songs every year.

YOU WILL NEED

> **paper**
> **pencil**
> **colored crayons**
> **binoculars**

1 To start with, draw a map of your wood. Then, early on in the year, just as the common resident birds start to call, get up early and look for them.

2 Male birds that are defending a territory will often sing from regular spots, called song perches. This could be the top of a tree or even a phone wire. All you have to do is identify it and mark on your map where you saw your bird singing. Over time you will find the perches of many birds in your woods.

3 Watch when they fly off and mark the direction and where they stopped on your map. Assuming your bird keeps to its territory, you will soon get a feel for what this is by his movements within it.

Take it further

* Look out for other birds of the same species. Other singing males nearby will be holding their own territories and you may be able to work out the boundaries if you watch and plot their movements on the map using a different color. If you can identify the females of a species, make notes of their movements as well.

* Keep this up for a few weeks and you will soon have a great journal of bird life in and around your woods. Keep watching through the year and you may be able to work out where the birds are nesting, how many chicks they raise and whether they have a second brood or not.

Talk with the birds

It's always a pleasure to interact with wildlife. Whether it's a pleasure for the wildlife is more doubtful. But as long as we don't overdo it, there is a lot that can be better understood by us trying.

Impersonating the calls of birds is a form of mimicry and a way to get to know bird song really well. With some species, it is possible to get the attention of the wild creatures themselves. That still leaves those of us that are not very good at mimicry in the dark, but fortunately there are a few bird songs that even those of us who are tone deaf and far from pitch perfect can master. These are birds that can be "called" by most of us.

Take my advice

While this is all good fun and a great educational experience, if it works, it is all the more tempting to keep calling the birds. But this is where a bit of respect needs to be applied. These animals are trying to get on with a life that is difficult enough without wasting loads of energy checking up on an apparent "intruder" in their patch, which is what you will sound like if you are doing it right! So once you have got the reaction you were looking for, it's only fair to leave the birds alone to get on with important stuff.

To attract a woodpecker, all you have to do is pretend to be another bird, which is as easy as finding a stick and whacking it against a good-sounding branch or tree trunk. Watch and wait and the local territory owner will come and check you out. If you hide yourself, you can even get it edging its way down the same tree you are hammering on.

Nick's tricks

* Here are two techniques that you can use at any time of year to entice birds to come to *you*. The first is called "pishing" and consists of making a repeated sound like "pssh-pssh-pssh-pssh." This imitates the alarm notes that several species of birds make when there is a hawk or other predator around. Instead of flying away, the other birds in the area come in to harass the supposed intruder—a behavior called mobbing. You can also make little squeaking sounds by kissing the back of your hand, which apparently attracts some birds out of sheer curiosity. You usually have to do these calls for a few minutes—and do them with confidence!—before they begin to work, but pretty soon you'll hear a bird or two, usually a chickadee, begin to respond. Sometimes it's possible to attract a flock of twenty birds of 5 or more species. And sometimes it's a complete bust. But when it works, it's awesome!

* Another trick to try is learning to imitate the call of an owl. This too stimulates the mobbing response described above. The wails and trills of the screech owl are the calls birders most often use. Listen to a CD of this call—you can probably find an audio of it on the internet—and then try to imitate it.

1 Having studied a chickadee's sound (see my trick, left), get a feel for it by "pishing" as loudly as you can. Do this through your hands in order to amplify the sound as much as possible.

2 Some owls' calls are best made by blowing through your upright thumbs, into cupped hands.

Nests and holes

During spring and summer, the woodlands and hedgerows are covered in leaves and birds carry out their daily lives more or less hidden from view. The whereabouts of birds and mammals are only given away by their occasional squeaks as young birds get stuffed with food, or a rustle as a squirrel leaps from branch to branch somewhere overhead in the canopy.

However, in the fall when the trees lose their leaves, all this changes, and in woods and hedgerows you will be able to see dense bundles of twigs and vegetation where birds built their nests. You may be able to find out where those birds you saw in the summer were living, or the nest might give you a clue about which birds live in that habitat.

At first, one nest may look very much like the next: just a tangle of sticks, straw, and mud. But with a little experience, a touch of guesswork and some persistence, you will be able to see that different birds construct different-looking nests.
> **Crows** make large, loose, stick nests.
> **American robins** make "adobe" bowls of vegetation cemented with mud.
> **Baltimore orioles** make hanging baskets woven of various fibers.

If you're really observant, in summer you can look out for the bored out nest holes created by woodpeckers. Different species create holes of different size, on trees of different ages, or even in different parts of the tree.

Take my advice

It is very important that you never disturb a bird's habitat, so always treat nests with respect and remember that it's best not to remove them from the place where you find them.

When looking for nests, it's not just the homes of birds that you are likely to come across. While scanning the tops of a woodland, you may well come across the summer drey of a gray squirrel, but the chances are that you wouldn't know you were looking at one. They resemble a hollowed-out crow's nest built high out on the branches. Much more distinctive is the dense winter drey that is also used as a nursery. These are often much larger and constructed with leafy twigs and lined with mosses and grass. They are also built close to the trunk where they are less prone to the buffeting of winter gales.

Take it further

* Once a nest has been used for one season it is rarely lived in again—well, at least not by creatures with feathers! So if you know of an empty nest, don't move it but take a good look inside. You might be surprised at the colony of little squatters that are present. The creatures that like to live in the leaf litter, such as woodlice, spiders, and multipedes, will think they have stumbled across a particularly neat equivalent of their usual habitat.

* You may also find various parasites of the birds that originally owned the nest, such as fleas, mites, and lice.

* Other creatures you could see include the moths that can get into your clothes or the beetles that can get into the carpet. In nature, these animals have an important role to play: they recycle keratin, the material that feathers and fur are made of, and of course, there is plenty of that in most nests.

You can look for the drey of the gray squirrel at any time of the year. They are, however, easier to see once all the leaves have fallen off in the winter.

Make your own nest

Birds' nests are real works of art, and different species construct their nests in various ways, using specific materials for the job. American robins are unusual among North American birds in having a hard lining of mud to their nests, while ruby-throated hummingbirds make a tiny cup of lichen flakes bound with spider webs. Some birds create very delicate constructions, while others look like a more messy pile of twigs. Some city-dwelling crows have even been known to make their nests from coathangers!

Why not try making your own nest? You will quickly see just what clever architects these birds are.

YOU WILL NEED

> **twigs and small sticks**
> **mud**
> **things to line your nest, such as hair of different types, grass and hay, feathers, moss, and leaves**

A bird's nest is a masterpiece of design, whatever the species.

1 Set aside a good space to work and gather your collection of materials.

2 Try to make a basic frame for your nest by using some of the sticks.

3 Add some mud to the frame to see if this helps stick everything together.

4 Gradually build up the nest with the softer materials, like hair and grass, to form a strong, solid structure capable of protecting fragile eggs and baby birds. Find a good location in a nearby hedge or tree. A bird may want to use your materials, or insects may decide they want to adopt your nest as their home!

Take it further

* Look at different hair. How does yours differ from a horse's or raccoon's?

* Different trees and shrubs produce very different sticks. Some are thinner and easier to bend than others—try them out and see what happens.

* To make this even more challenging, find out how a particular species constructs its nest and try to copy it in style, using only the materials it uses. Can you do such a neat job?

Bridging the gaps

Between woods and fields there is often a dense tangle of bushes and scrub, a kind of transition area between two very different habitats. It's certainly not a field, but it's also not a full grown forest. Such places are called *ecotones* and are often jumping with wildlife because creatures from both the bordering fields and forests use them—and they also have species that live just in the scrub itself.

Find a patch of shrub-scrub near you—a power line cut is a good place to look—and get to know it. Listen for the distinctive songs of prairie warblers and field sparrows and see how many different butterflies you can identify; successional areas usually have a big variety of the plants that caterpillars prefer as food.

Changes in vegetation on the landscape, called *succession,* can tell you a lot about the history of your neighborhood. The presence of mature red cedar for example often indicates an area of poor soil that was cleared for grazing sheep or cattle a hundred years ago or more and then abandoned. Places dominated by huckleberry scrub and bracken fern typically show where there has been a fire.

Nick's trick

* The leaves of plants in successional areas get eaten by lots of different animals. To protect themselves against these plant munchers (herbivores), they have developed chemicals in their tissues that taste bad and, to advertize this, they give off a strong smell (and taste!) when chewed. Try crushing a leaf from a variety of different plants in a scrubby area in your neighborhood and sniffing the juice. You could try mature red cedar, huckleberry scrub, bracken fern, buckthorn, honeysuckle (pictured above), and Asian honeysuckle. Some will smell just, well, "planty," but you may be surprised at how many have a strong smell all their own. It is amazing how different some plants can smell compared with others.

WARNING: Watch out for poison ivy! Be super sure you know what poison ivy looks like before you go squishing leaves, as otherwise you might have a very unpleasant shock! And whatever you do, don't try tasting any of them...

Disturbed areas—places where vegetation has been cleared and the ground dug up—can also encourage the growth and spread of invasive plants that are not native to your area. When a species arrives in a place where it has never been before, it is sometimes able to behave in ways that it wasn't allowed to previously where there were local predators and other factors that controlled its population.

Invasive plants are not bad because they are foreign—many of our favorite wild flowers came from Europe with early colonists and are popular with native butterflies. But a few aggressive species such as Asian honeysuckles, buckthorns, barberries, and bittersweet can take over an area, drive out native species and create a sterile habitat where local birds and other species can no longer live.

YOU WILL NEED

> **tape measure**
> **pencil and paper**
> **field guide**

1 Locate two different looking scrubby areas, one pretty wild-looking, the other more tame. Then mark off a 50 foot long section of each.

2 Using a field guide and a pencil and paper, record the number of different plant species that you find in each area. You may want to visit your plots several times at different seasons to get the most complete list.

3 When you think you have pretty complete lists, count the species and identify which are native and which are not. (Your field guide should tell you this.) Divide the number of non-native species by the *total* number of species to find the *percentage* of non-natives in each plot. Which plot has the highest number of total species and the most aggressive invasives?

Seed watching!

I know watching seeds sounds like an activity that is about as exciting as watching paint dry and grass grow, but bear with me, there is a point to all this—and that is, ANTS. These small, but important creatures are very good at clearing up the place, but they are also gardeners. Remember those slow-growing, slow to colonize woodland flowers such as lilies and violets (see page 11)? Well, both of these plants rely on the valuable courier services of ants to shift their seeds about on the woodland floor.

Fab facts

Have a good look around the base of a violet and you may find some small little flower heads, which are there as a backup. They contain seeds that do not need insects to pollinate or carry them. So just in case the insects do not do their job properly, there will still be violets next year. This is also the reason they can exist in dense clumps.

1 In the summer, collect some ripe seeds of various flowers. I find those little plastic film canisters are really handy for this as they are dark and airtight. If you don't have any, ask at your local photo-developing shop.

2 Then find the ants—it shouldn't be too hard, they are never very far away. If you find a colony or a trail that are foraging, tip out your seeds in a pile and watch what happens. Do the ants show an interest in your seeds?

3 What you may see is that some seeds have a "handle" on them, which contain substances such as oils and proteins, which the ants are fond of. So they pick up the whole thing and carry it off, providing a very valuable delivery service for the otherwise slow-to-disperse plant. Back at the nest, the handle is chewed off and the very hard seed discarded.

Take it further

Try out other seeds on your ants. Does the type of seed make a difference? Do different types of ant prefer one seed to another?

The herb layer

In the herb layer, plants may seem a little stunted compared to the towering woodland giants above them. But the "herb" layer of woodland is, in fact, very important. It's a fuzzy layer of the woodland that sometimes blurs into the understory. But if it wasn't there, much of the spirit of woodland would be missed, such as the great floral spectaculars of trilliums, violets, and wood anemone.

Many of the butterflies that sail upon the calm air of woodland glades and clearings are fed by the grasses and the other succulent plants that form the herb layer when the butterflies are caterpillars.

This layer is most obvious in the places where the greatest amount of sunlight hits the ground: such as woodland edges, rides, along paths and in clearings. Here the Sun's energy allows a variety of plants to grow and if you are looking for insects and flowers, this is the best place to start.

Because light is the limiting factor on the woodland floor, many plants that live in deciduous woodlands (those whose leaves drop off in winter) have a life cycle that is tuned into the seasons. This is why plants such as forest lilies and violets put on such a big show in the early part of the year. This is practically the only time in the year they get any light before the trees' leaves unfurl and block out the sunlight.

Raccoons den in hollow logs, rock crevices, and other cavities during the day, but forage on the forest floor at night in search of anything edible including nuts, fruits, and insects.

Colorful soldier beetles are relatives of fireflies. Several species feed on pollen, nectar, and small insects like aphids in the herb layer.

In woods without the dense herb layer, you lose the diversity of animals on the floor itself. But this does allow you to see evidence of the activities of other animals clearly: in this case, some squirrel nibbled cones.

Where the sunlight can reach the woodland floor, such as where a tree has fallen, a great lush carpet of plant life can thrive.

See the light

One way that scientists measure and record plants is by using something called a transect. This is simply a line or a piece of string stretched from one place to another. It might not sound that exciting, but a transect can tell you an awful lot, especially if you stretch it across a path, clearing, or woodland ride. Make sure you choose one that isn't busy, otherwise people, dogs, and horses will keep getting tangled up. They will then get cross with you and you won't learn anything apart from a few new curses!

By making a transect you will start to get to know your flowering plants well, and that in itself is very satisfying. Take along a good field guide and try to identify what you come across. If you cannot identify any plants while you are there, you could always pop a few leaves of the plant that is causing you an identification problem in a plastic bag, label it, and try again at home later. You may even want to record your findings permanently by "pressing" leaves and flowers and keeping a journal of your findings (see page 14).

Fab fact

Skunk cabbage is one of the strangest plants growing in wet woods. It is often the first plant to appear in the spring because its odd-looking flowers actually generate heat! As the name implies, the flowers give off a stinky smell. This attracts flies and beetles that also feed on dead animals. Tricking these insects in this way is the skunk cabbage's clever method of ensuring that it is pollinated.

YOU WILL NEED

> **2 poles (bamboo, sticks or pegs)**
> **long length of string**
> **level**
> **measuring stick/tape**
> **numerous lengths of short string (depending on the length of the transect line)**
> **graph paper**
> **pencil**

1 To set up your transect line, stretch your length of string between two poles at either end of the survey line. Make sure the string is above the highest vegetation and use the level to check that it is level before continuing.

2 To make things a little easier, mark or tie every 3 feet a short length of string. On the graph paper, mark the length of your transect line, and each 3 foot interval. This will be the horizontal axis, showing how far along the line each plant is.

3 Record the height of your end poles. On your graph, the height will be the ends of your vertical axis. At the end of the project this will show the heights of the plants inbetween.

4 Work your way along the line, measuring at each marked interval the distance between the string and the tips of every plant. Record this together with the species of each plant if possible.

Take it further

* Once you have recorded on your paper the heights of all these plants, you will start to get an interesting profile. The plants' height and growth vary depending upon where they grow in relation to the tree canopy above. Could this have something to do with available light?

* Look at the species found in different places. Do you think some are better suited to grow in the shade than others? Maybe some of these plants do not like being disturbed. If you are on a footpath that is used a lot, maybe some plants simply do not like getting walked all over!

Small game hunting

Just how good are you at sneaking up on things without them sensing you? Well, this art is called field craft and it is one of the most useful skills you can have as a naturalist. If you see yourself as a bit of a master in the skills of moving with stealth, then there are a few fun ways to test yourself. The first is in the form of a game.

The object is to make an obstacle course that is as noisy as possible. Try doing this in your local woodland. Find a patch with lots of dead twigs or leaves, or make your own course in your garden. You can use rustly paper, potato chip packets, dry twigs, or leaves. Be sure to clean up after you finish your game.

1 With the help of a few friends, select a "rabbit." This is the person who has to use their ears. Stand your rabbit at one end of your rustle zone, facing away from you and wearing a blindfold.

2 Now take turns to try to stalk towards your friend, without him hearing your movements. Your aim is to approach so close you can touch the "rabbit" without him hearing you. You have three lives and lose one every time the rabbit hears you and points directly at where you are standing.

Take it further

You can make up the rules, also, such as adding obstacles to climb over or under to make things really difficult, or you can try going barefoot or with shoes on. See how well you do.

Now, this isn't the end of your master class at field craft. The biggest test of all is a real animal, and you do not get anything more nervous than a woodchuck. They have sensitive ears and they are very untrusting. You do not get to be a successful woodchuck in any other way!

1 Find a field at the edge of a woodland, ideally a place where you have seen woodchucks before. Once you've located your animal, watch it for a while and see if you can discover where the entrance to its den is located.

2 Wear clothes that are not too bright, preferably greens and browns that match the habitat. Then get down on your belly and see how close you can get to the woodchuck before it bolts for its hole.

3 When it does this—as it surely will—use the opportunity to move close to the hole, perhaps ten feet to one side. Woodchucks are very curious and if you lie still it may come back out and start feeding again right in front of you! But you have to stay really still and be really patient.

How to hide yourself

"Slowly, quietly, into the breeze" is the most basic mantra for a naturalist, and it is a skill that can be used and applied in any habitat, anywhere in the world. What this doesn't take into account, however, is the "outline" or shape of the naturalist. You need to use as much of the natural cover as possible and that means playing hide and seek!

Keep low and hidden, or at least make sure your silhouette is not seen. You can be as quiet as you like, wearing the very latest in camouflage gear, but if you break the horizon, the animals will see you, smell you, and be off like a shot!

One of the most useful things you can do, especially if you want to spend some time observing a creature, is to build a blind. Now this can be done in many ways. One of my favorite blinds as a child was a large cardboard box. It allowed me to get really close to rabbits, and then to the bird table in my garden, and eventually it enabled me to watch a fox hunting rabbits and a buzzard feeding on a dead sheep! Get a box that is large enough for you to fit comfortably inside. Take some scissors and cut out viewing slots, one on each of the four sides is best, as then you do not have any blind spots. If you want to sit in it in the rain, coat it with water-based varnish or even glue to prolong its life for a couple of months. If you don't want to sit in a box for hours, see opposite.

The simplest and most portable blind is to buy a sheet of scrim (that's the netting with the green and brown bits of plastic attached to it). The army uses it and you can get it quite cheaply from an army surplus store. Throw this stuff over you or peg it up in the bushes to form an instant hideout. Or you can build one out of natural materials in the area, bending branches and tying ferns and other vegetation to it to camouflage yourself.

2

Take a third cane and tie it with string so that it joins together the two standing canes. Tie them together as near to the top as possible.

3

Push two more canes into the ground 3 feet behind the first two and continue to join the remaining canes around the top to form a kind of empty cube.

1

Stick two of the bamboo canes in the ground, about 3 feet apart. Push them in far enough so that they stay put.

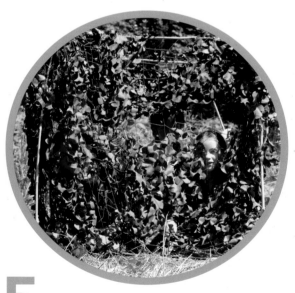

4

Stand back and admire your work. But it's not much of a hide like this—it's definitely missing something.

5

Throw the scrim over the top so that it covers all four sides. Climb inside and keep watch.

Beaver watch

Everyone knows what a beaver looks like, but have you ever actually watched one in the wild? When the first Europeans came to America, beavers became one of the colonists' biggest exports because of their beautiful and warm fur. Soon they were almost extinct. But within the last 50 years they have made a big comeback and have gotten to be quite common. Beavers are among the few animals that—like us—actually make their own habitat. Watching them create and maintain their water park in the woods is incredibly interesting.

The first thing to do is to find some likely beaver habitat. Though we rightly think of beavers as being water-loving creatures, they are just as accurately described as woodland animals. In order to construct their dams and lodges they need wood and their favorite trees are slender fast growing species like poplar, birch, and willow. Look for wooded areas near you that look flooded with dead or living trees standing in the water—often a clue that beavers have been at work.

Beavers are attracted by the sound of running water. This tells them where they need to build their dams in order to make a beaver pond. They begin by plugging up the stream with all kinds of stuff—sticks, leaves, grass, and mud—until the land upstream of the new dam begins to flood. Then the whole beaver family—except

Beavers are large members of the rodent family—you could describe them as giant, water-loving mice! Their big, flat tails have many uses. They use them as rudders and "sculling oars" in the water and for balance when foraging on land. The tail also stores fat for the long winters and can help regulate body temperature.

Take my advice

One of the other creatures that beavers make new habitat for is mosquitoes, and the best beaver-watching hours are also prime mosquito time. But this need not spoil your beaver watch. Just be sure to wear long pants and a long-sleeved shirt.

the youngest, called "kits"—put more and more sticks over the edge of the widening flow until the water has risen to the height they prefer. Some dams are as much as 10 feet high, but most are about 3 feet.

To find the center of beaver activity, look for a big (5–6 foot high) mound of sticks and mud in the middle of an area of water. This is the "lodge" where the beaver family lives summer and winter. Once you've spotted the lodge, try to find a dry spot with a little height where you can watch the beavers coming and going. Beavers are largely nocturnal (active at night), but in the summer they start working in the early evening when there is still light in the sky and are usually still at it near sunrise. These are the best times to find your spot and watch.

The beaver's reputation for industriousness ("busy as a beaver") is well-deserved. Take your field notebook along on your beaver watch and record the details of the beavers' activity. How much time do they spend gathering materials, maintaining the dam, feeding, remaining inside the lodge? How do they interact with each other?

The lodge is usually begun on a raised area on the pond bottom in relatively shallow water. As the walls are built up above the waterline with sticks, sod, and mud a space in the center is kept hollow. This "living room" is about 7 feet wide and 2 feet high and has a dry (well, pretty dry!) floor with a carpet of grass, moss, and wood chips.

Take it further

* Make a map of the beaver pond, showing the location of the dam, lodge, and other prominent features of the area the beavers have created. Can you figure out what the place might have looked like before the beavers flooded it?

* In addition to creating a home for themselves, beavers create new habitats for a wide variety of other plants and animals such as dragonflies and even Great Blue Herons that build their nests in the dead trees that were drowned by the flooding. Make a list of the species that benefit from the beavers presence and draw some of them in your notebook. Is there a "downside" to the beaver activity?

Know your cones

We have so far talked about seeds, nuts, and berries, but what about conifers, or members of the pine family, as they are otherwise known? Well, the seeds of these are packaged into neat little devices that we all know as cones. Cones are beautiful, simple, and functional little seed "shakers."

Pine trees do not rely on an agent like a bird or a mammal to do the distributing of the future generations for them. Instead, they rely on the wind to scatter them. To see what I mean, collect some pine cones that are closed and sealed and take them home to hang up in a warm, dry place. Watch what happens as the cones dry out. The scales that make up the cone's body start to open and as they do this, the insides are exposed: the seeds.

So if there is good dry weather, it is perfect for making seeds that will blow around and not get stuck to things. But that isn't enough. A few of those seeds will fall out, as you may see if you place a piece of white paper below the cones and give them a shake. Just like a salt pot, the cones give up many of their papery scales, each a "wing" for the tiny little seed. In the wild, this makes total sense. Seeds not only need dry weather to blow around, they also need a breeze and the cone will not release its seeds until it is buffeted about a bit.

Maple keys (left) and cone seeds (far left) are lightweight and designed to twirl or fly in the breeze so they can travel away from "home."

Look for the "keys" or helicopter seeds of maple and ash. They are called helicopters for a good reason. Pick some and throw them up in the air. They are designed to rotate, slowing their fall, as the longer it takes to fall, the farther away from the mother tree the seeds will travel. This is a good idea if the seeds want to get away from the shadow of the mother tree and also avoid competition with her roots for water and minerals.

When out in your woodland, look out for other trees that ride the breeze in a similar way. In the spring, willows and poplars produce white fluffy seeds that can sometimes blow around in such numbers it can look like a late snow storm!

These hazel catkins are the male part of the tree's flowers. Crumple them between your fingers and look at what they are made of— neat little stacks of winged seeds.

Spore points

If you look carefully enough at a mushroom, you can identify many species by the color, texture, and shape of the cap. But have you yet had a peek at what's going on underneath? It is here that the millions of spores are produced from structures that are not only very beautiful, but also can be characteristic of the species of fungus. To explore further, follow the steps opposite. Here is a great blend of art and appreciation of nature combined with the science of getting to know your fungi even more intimately. Many fungi are poisonous. So, if you touch ANY fungus, do not rub your eyes or touch your face afterwards. Make sure you also wash your hands thoroughly.

Look again at the surface under the mushroom. It is made up of either gills or pores and when dry, this surface will shed their living dust: the spores (see also page 62).

What you will see if you have been successful with your project is the pattern of the gills or pores made up by the millions of microscopic spores that have lain exactly where they have fallen. Before long the pattern will get disrupted as they blow around, so if you wish to keep your spore print, spray it with fixative (available from all good art suppliers). If this is hard to get hold of, a can of hairspray will be just as good.

This tree is in the process of being digested from the insides out by honey fungus. Most of its life, though, you would hardly know it was there as it lives in the soil and wood of its victims.

Fab facts

* Hidden from the naked eye, the underground threads of just a little clump of the common honey fungus could stretch for over 15 hectares, weigh over 100 tons, and be 1,500 years old.

* To get a glimpse of the secret world of fungi, peel up an old dead leaf, lift a piece of bark or dig with your fingers into the leaf litter, and you will find yellow to white threads spreading like veins—these are the usually unseen parts of a fungus.

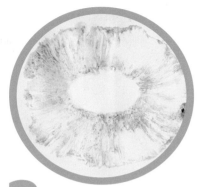

1 Take the sharp knife and cut through the stem of the fungus, flush with the underside of its cap. Do this very gently and so as not to damage any of the spore structures. Turn the cap over so the sporing surface is face down on a piece of heavy paper. Cover with a bowl to stop the air blowing the spores around.

2 Leave for a day or so before lifting the bowl and the fungus off the paper. What do you see? A lovely imprint of the fungus's gills.

Take it further

* So if the mushroom or toadstool is the fungus equivalent of a fruit, then where is the rest of it? For the most part it is right below your feet. If you were able to put on special x-ray specs that allow you to see through things and pick up only fungi, then you would be in for a shock. It is only where the threads weave together and pop up to the surface of the forest floor or tree bark that we actually see the fungus that we are familiar with.

* Still wearing your x-ray specs, look down and every dead leaf and rotting branch would be a dense mass, like a huge, thick cobweb of tentacles, each one slowly digesting the dead stuff of both animals and plants.

* Look up and the network of threads of other species will be spreading through some of the living tissues of the trees.

The litter layer

When we refer to the litter layer, this isn't meant in a derogatory way, it's just referring to the position that this habitat holds within the woodland. It is a deep slice of rich, dark, decaying leaves and wood, natural mulch, and fertilizer for the trees above and every other plant that lives under their spreading canopy.

Get down and have a close look, and as you dig through the litter, you travel back in time. The leaf litter starts at the top with the most recently fallen leaves and as you dig deeper, you start to find small creatures that recycle the leaves by eating them. In turn, they provide food for predatory creatures that also lurk there.

Go deeper still and you will start to see the "tentacles" of fungi and slime molds and eventually you get to see the product of their recycling work. The composters have done just that—they have turned the leaves into fertilizer.

There are probably more creatures and other organisms here than anywhere else in the woodlands. They are always kept in employment as every acre of deciduous woodland can drop half a ton of leaves on the soil beneath. With a meal like that, the recyclers have to be extremely numerous indeed!

To see more of what I mean, take a white tray or piece of white paper and toss a handful of leaf litter smack in the middle of it and watch. In a few minutes, a parade of creatures will start to leave the security of the moldering mass. Everything from minuscule springtails to big predatory beetles will appear. Use a field guide to help you identify what it is that you are looking at.

Just because they're little, it doesn't mean they're not ferocious. This ground beetle is the lion of the leaf litter, actively running down their prey.

A world under your feet. We walk all over it, but rarely give it the attention it deserves.

Spend some time rummaging around and you can find everything from mini-monsters to the tell-tale signs of other woodland creatures.

Signs and reading them right

Spend enough time in the woods and you will start to notice that old stumps and fallen branches are often used by animals as places to process their food. They become tables, handy spots to sit and eat at, and also lookout posts from which they can keep a wary and watchful eye on the surroundings—just in case. Even a predator like a hawk has enemies to watch for when it's on the ground.

So, what should you be keeping an eye open for? First, there are plucking posts, which are places where a bird of prey such as a sharp-shinned hawk will take its kill— say, a song sparrow—and, literally, pluck it. Sharp-shinned hawks specialize in catching birds and often return to the same plucking posts. Once you have found one, you can return and find the remains of other species of bird—a good way to start a feather collection.

Or, if you find a lot of feathers in one place, it's a sure sign that some bird somewhere got unlucky. The possible scenarios are that it died naturally and was scavenged or it was killed by either a bird or a mammal. However, just because one animal killed it, doesn't mean that something else didn't scavenge the remains.

Often, the best a naturalist can do is figure out if the bird was eaten by a predatory bird or by a mammal, and this is actually quite easy. Birds of prey, like hawks, tend to kill birds and get straight down to business, eating from the breast area first. Small birds are often totally consumed, but larger birds can be nearly intact except for a hole in their chest. You may also notice little triangular nicks in the breast bone where the beak of the bird of prey removed chunks of meat.

Trunks and stumps are worth checking for feeding signs. Bark with fissures is often used as an anvil by woodpeckers and nuthatches; the wedged-in nut fragments can be seen still jammed in place. Here, I'm looking at a plucking post, where a hawk has eaten a small bird.

The big feathers can also be a clue: they would have been gripped by the narrow hooked beak and torn from the unfortunate victim's body. Look closely and you may well notice a bend or kink in the main feather shaft.

A bird that has been eaten by a mammal, on the other hand, will be a much messier job. Bundles of feathers will be stuck together by saliva or sheared off at the base.

Also, scuffle around on the woodland floor or at the base of shrubbery and you will not only find the recyclers but the tracks and signs left by many woodland creatures. Under the influence of gravity, everything that drops in a woodland ends up here, on the floor. Feathers, egg shells, seeds, fruit, droppings, and pellets; it really is rich pickings for the sharp-eyed naturalist. So get out there and get on your hands and knees!

The habitat at the base of a tree can be a good starting point for seeking out signs of life. Many small animals like moving around edges next to cover and birds will sometimes leave pellets and droppings here as well.

Nick's trick

As you start to get to know your woodland well, add these sorts of details to a map of the area.

Woodpecker droppings—I'm talking about those species that feed a lot on ants, such as flickers and pileated. Their droppings look a little like cigarette ash. Crumble a dry one between your fingers and investigate with a magnifying lens. You will see the remains of the hard bits of ants' bodies.

Nuts—who has nibbled them?

The majority of wild mammals are next to impossible to see; the best you can expect is a fleeting glimpse of a furry backside vanishing in to a thicket while you are out walking. But this is where mere mortals give up and good naturalists find a way. We simply become detectives, and many a scientific survey has been carried out on the secret activities of the furry ones by simply looking for and at the signs they leave behind.

You might think that the smaller the mammal, the fewer traces they leave behind. Footprints and droppings can be hard to come by, of course, but those mammals that like to sink their teeth into the soft kernels of nuts and seeds—particularly those of hazel trees—leave behind some very obvious traces.

The best time of the year to look for feeding signs of our small mammals is in the fall, when acorns and other nuts tend to be fresh and any that have been chewed open by small rodents will practically shout at you! Their white or green broken remains seem to almost glow in the dim recesses of the hedgerow. But having said that, nuts and seeds are hard and stick around for a while before they start to rot, so keep an eye out at anytime.

A handful of evidence. These nut cases have been opened and eaten by woodland mammals. Can you tell by whom? Those on the right were split down the middle by a squirrel and those on the left were worked by the smaller teeth of a wood mouse.

Take it further

Use a hand lens to have a good look at the surface around the nut's hole. Here you will find teeth marks and these will give you some idea of how the animal opens and eats the kernel inside. Each species has its own technique. What the inside of the lip of the opening looks like is also helpful.

* **Squirrels** are fairly destructive. Using their incisors, they first take a notch out of one end of the nut and then split the nut into two halves.
* **Mice** hold the nut and use their upper teeth to grip while the lower ones gnaw.
* **Voles** make a hole, stick their nose in and do the opposite thing, gripping on the inside and gnawing from the outside.

The best place to look for nut remains is often—surprisingly—nowhere near the nut trees! You have to think like a small mammal here. They like to feed and run in relative security as they are a highly desirable meal for many other creatures in the woodland. So scavenge around in the leaf litter and under roots, stones, and logs near a tree and you will start to uncover evidence of who lives there.

Other nuts you may find on your explorations may be jammed into the crevices in tree bark. They are usually left there by birds, especially by nuthatches (hence their name) and woodpeckers. They jam the nut into place and then hammer at it with their beak. The woodpeckers almost always put the nuts in the right way up and they have favorite places to work, so you may notice a pile of split nut shells below. Nuthatches, on the other hand, have smaller, less powerful beaks and knock a small hole in the outer shell. They also do not often re-use their sites and so leave the nut shells in position once they have taken the kernel.

The number one cone crunchers are squirrels—they hold the cone top down and start at the cone's base, gnawing off the scales and eating the energy-rich seeds as they go. Sometimes you will find them at tree stump "tables," which provide a useful perch, giving the animals a small height advantage, allowing them to see any approaching predators.

The fungus among us

In your average deciduous woodland there may be around 100 million leaves for every acre of land, and at the end of the year these will all come tumbling down to lie on the forest floor as leaf litter—almost 2 tons of it per acre in fact.

This quantity of leaf litter represents a huge pile of eating to anything that can digest cellulose; that's the hard stuff that makes wood "woody." Cellulose is also contained in leaves. Few living things can eat it, but this is where bacteria and fungi come in—and what a good job they do, too. They must do, otherwise we would all be up to our necks in rotting leaves!

Bacteria are too small to see, but fungi can be found most of the year round, becoming most visible in the autumn. It is when it's damp that those beautiful and weird structures we know as mushrooms suddenly appear. These do the same job as the seed heads of many true plants. But instead of dispersing seeds, they send out tiny little packages of life called spores.

So now it is time to get to know them better. Start by going on a fungus foray with a field guide and see how many of these mushrooms you can find. You can even try preserving some of them and keeping a collection. But how do you keep such juicy and complex structures? Well, there are some fungi that will dissolve to mush almost as soon as you look at them, but most can be baked in a sand tray—which removes the water from the fungus (see opposite).

The job of that classic mushroom shape is to keep the spore-bearing surfaces—the gills and pores that can be found on the underside—in good working order. This means protecting their delicate surfaces from the weather and the rain.

Fab fact

A simple 4 inch wide mushroom can have over 600 million spores inside it.

YOU WILL NEED

> **a couple of baking trays**
> **some fine sand**
> **some fungus**
> **large serving spoon**

1 Fill one of the baking trays with the sand and bake in the oven at 230°F for a few hours. Then carefully remove from the oven using oven gloves.

2 Carefully spoon half of the hot sand into the second baking tray and gently put your fungus on top of it.

3 Spoon in the rest of the hot sand, brushing it into all crevices until your fungi are totally immersed. Leave for a day before checking your fungi. If not totally dry, repeat until all the moisture is absorbed by the sand.

Take my advice

Many fungi are poisonous. So, if you touch ANY fungus, do not rub your eyes or touch your face afterwards. Make sure you also wash your hands thoroughly.

Take it further

The fungi are then ready for storage or presenting. To ensure your treasures last for a long time, store them in an airtight container with packets of drying agents such as silica gel. This can be bought from electrical equipment and photographic shops.

Boring beetles

Beetles are not boring in the "dull" sense of the word, but it's a good description of the lives they lead or, rather, the lives that some of their grubs lead. Look at dead wood closely—either fallen branches or on the trunks themselves—and you will almost certainly notice holes!

Many of these are made by insects, the beetles being some of the most noticeable culprits. The most beautiful works of art are those made by the bark beetles. You may notice on dead trees, where the bark has fallen away, that there are some strange squiggles. These are the tunnels of bark beetles and there are many different kinds, each one making their own distinctive pattern.

The adult beetles, which you would be very lucky to see, meet and mate in a small chamber under the bark. The female then digs a tunnel of her own along which she lays her eggs.

When the tree is living, this is what you would see underneath the bark. The white grubs have eaten their way out from the center, where their mother laid her eggs.

When an old fallen tree starts to rot and its bark falls off, look on the smooth wood underneath for the galleries of bark beetles.

Nick's trick

If you want to preserve the patterns of these tiny creatures' work, it is easy enough to make a rubbing or a cast in the same way as you cast or made rubbings of bark on pages 16 and 17.

On hatching, the larvae munch their way outward through the relatively soft dead wood and finally pupate at the end. Their entire journey is represented by the radiating spokes of the design. If you look carefully at the bark, assuming it is still in place, you should be able to see the little exit holes by which the newly hatched beetles left! These beetles are quite common, so take time to hunt around beech, elm, oak, and pine trees.

You may also find other holes and dents in dead wood, as many other insects, including the large stag beetles, click beetles, long-horn beetles, termites, ants, and even the caterpillars of some moths, will also consume the wood. If you examine dead logs, you may find the larvae of these. When doing this, notice how robust and chunky their mouth parts are.

An elm bark beetle going about its work.

Galling

Oak apples, robin's pin cushions, artichokes, and spangles are all great folk names for galls. These are the little life-support capsules created by the "irritation" caused to a plant by the presence of the egg or grub of many species of tiny wasps and flies. You can find a vast number of different types in any woodland.

Even though you probably won't easily be able to see the tiny adult insect in the wild, there are ways you can meet them. Having said that, the actual architecture of the galls themselves and the life cycle are probably far more interesting to the young naturalist.

Just take your average oak tree. If you were to search every inch of its living surface (and I mean below ground on the roots too), you could find more than 40 different species of gall. Despite the large numbers of galls present, they don't seem to do the tree any real harm.

Here's an experiment you can try over the winter to hatch a gall wasp. In the fall, you first need to collect some galls with no exit holes. (If they do have exit holes, the galls have probably fulfilled their purpose and the insect has already checked

Nick's trick

Many of these galls have been home to more than one insect. A visual way of showing just how many is by putting a pin in each hole as you count.

out.) The best ones to collect are the apple galls from the twigs of oak trees. Or use little spangle galls, which look like "flying saucers" attached to the undersides of leaves of the same tree. Now follow the steps below, remembering that you won't see the results for several months.

1 Place the galls in a large clear plastic bag together with some straw. Pop a drinking straw in the top, blow into it to inflate the bag, and tie shut with string.

2 Sit back and wait for the little wasps, all female, to appear near the top of the bag. Some will hatch early due to temperature change, but keep them cool and most will hatch in the spring. Set the wasps free after the hatch.

Take it further

If you want a more instant insight into the world of the gall wasp, look for empty "oak apples," which are some of the biggest around. Then use a sharp knife to cut them in half to see what goes on inside. You will notice that the grub eats its own surroundings—it lives in its dinner until it is ready to emerge as an adult insect.

Little jumpers

Crickets and grasshoppers are familiar insects in many habitats but I include them here because it is in the bushier habitats that the aptly named bush crickets can be found. If we are going to talk about crickets, then we almost certainly have to talk about the grasshoppers that will be found chirping and chirruping in the grassy fields and shrubby woodland edges.

Catching and collecting crickets can be something of a sport because they really are tricky little jumpers. So, for this particular sport, I have invented cricket tongs. I call them this, but they are just as useful for catching any small animal that sits on foliage and is of a nervous disposition. Picture this: your intended subject of study, a nervous bush cricket, sits sunbathing on a leaf. You make a lunge for it, the whole bush gets snagged on your sweater and your prey detects the commotion and hops off! But armed with cricket tongs—well, success on a stick!

Take it further

How do crickets and grasshoppers make their "music"? Everyone knows that. They rub their legs together, right? *Wrong!* Crickets make some amazingly loud sounds by rubbing a tiny scraper on the edge of one wing against an equally minute serrated ridge on the other wing—kind of like running your finger along the teeth of a comb. The sound is amplified by a kind of sound chamber formed by the upraised wings. If you sneak up carefully on a "fiddling" cricket, you can actually watch them doing this! Grasshoppers make more raspy sounds by rubbing a spiny leg against papery wings. Crickets and grasshoppers are closely related and are incredibly important because they eat huge amounts of grass and other plants and in turn are a major food item for many other animals.

1 Using a good length of duct tape, attach one of the tea strainers to the end of one of the pieces of garden cane.

2 Using a second piece of duct tape, attach the other end of the stick to the end of one half of the barbeque tongs.

3 Repeat with the other strainer and stick, making sure the strainers align to create a ball-shaped insect grabber. You now have the perfect device for catching your best friend or …

4 … with a stealthy approach and a bit of practice, you should be able to bag many a cricket, grasshopper, or any other nervous insect.

5 Carefully transfer anything you catch to a clear plastic container and then you can study it with a magnifying glass before setting it free again.

Going further

This book was never meant to be anything but the very beginning of a journey—I see it as being the map, the compass, and a kick in the right direction. As you continue to various forests and woods, you will begin to ask more questions and discover things that this book may not be able to answer. This is why this section exists—to give you a few more pointers in the right direction.

Good reading

National Geographic My First Pocket Guide Series (Age 6-10)
> *Backyard Wilderness*
> *Garden Birds*
> *Insects*
> *Reptiles & Amphibians*

National Audubon Society First Field Guides
> *Amphibians*
> *Birds*
> *Insects*
> *Trees*

Peterson Field Guides for Young Naturalists (Age 8-12)
> *Backyard Birds*
> *Butterflies*
> *Caterpillars*
> *Songbirds*
> *Wildflowers*

Stokes Beginner's Guides
> *Birds (Eastern)*
> *Birds (Western)*
> *Bats*
> *Bird Feeding*

> *Butterflies*
> *Hummingbirds*
See also American Birding Association on-line catalog for additional birding books aimed at kids.

Handy organizations

Audubon Societies: There are several tiers of Audubon Societies including the National Audubon Society, which has chapters in many states and large independent Audubon Societies such as Mass Audubon and New Jersey Audubon. Most of these organizations have many programs and sometimes publications for young naturalists.

Defenders of Wildlife: This national conservation organization publishes a well-known magazine for young naturalists called *Ranger Rick*.

Special Interest Clubs: Many states and provinces have clubs devoted to the study of specific taxa: wildflowers, bats, butterflies, etc., and of course birds. These are way too numerous to list here. These clubs are usually glad to have kids come along on field trips. The best way to find these in your area is to go on line and "google" your favorite subject, like "Virginia butterfly club" and see what you get.

Handy stuff – equipment supplies and other contacts

Carolina Biological Supply Company
- www.carolina@carolina.com

Ward's Natural Science
P.O. Box 92912
Rochester, NY 14892-9012
www.wardsci.com

BioQuip Products
2321 Gladwick St.
Rancho Dominguez, CA -90220
www.bioquip.com

The first two are large national companies that have segments specializing in equipment and publications for kids. BioQuip specializes in insect equipment and publications.

Index

Author's acknowledgments

> Big thanks to the energetic and hardworking team at HarperCollins who put this book together. Especially the tireless Helen Brocklehurst—how she holds everything together when it comes to building books, I don't know. But thankfully she does and she's good at it. And the same for Emma Callery, who as editor for this book has endured the frustrating half-finished manuscripts, bad grammar and spelling and, of course, the continual frustration of not being able to get hold of me on the phone! Thanks for not shouting at me and getting cross! Nikki English, the photographer, who has the patience of a saint and found the energy to continue wrangling animals and children both at the same time, AND managing to take great photographs; surely the definition of multi-tasking!

> The Devon Wildlife Trust for letting us take photographs in the very beautiful Dunsford woods.
> The children—Barney, Hattie, Jed, Lucy, and Millie—for all their patience with us and the props, cameras, and animals. I would especially like to thank Barney for reminding me what it was like to be a young naturalist.
> Chris Leahy at Massachusetts Audubon for invaluable advice.